Mathematical Thinking at Grade 5

INTRODUCTION
LANDMARKS IN THE NUMBER SYSTEM

TERC

Investigations in Number, Data, and Space®

Dale Seymour Publications®

Menlo Park, California

The *Investigations* curriculum was developed at TERC (formerly
Technical Education Research Centers) in collaboration with Kent State
University and the State University of New York at Buffalo. The work was
supported in part by National Science Foundation Grant No. ESI-9050210.
TERC is a nonprofit company working to improve mathematics and science
education. TERC is located at 2067 Massachusetts Avenue, Cambridge,
MA 02140.

**This project was supported, in part,
by the**
National Science Foundation
Opinions expressed are those of the authors
and not necessarily those of the Foundation

Managing Editor: Catherine Anderson
Series Editor: Beverly Cory
Manuscript Editor: Karen Becker
ESL Consultant: Nancy Sokol Green
Production/Manufacturing Director: Janet Yearian
Production/Manufacturing Coordinator: Joe Conte
Design Manager: Jeff Kelly
Design: Don Taka
Illustrations: DJ Simison, Carl Yoshihara
Composition: Archetype Book Composition

This book is published by Dale Seymour Publications®, an imprint of
Addison Wesley Longman, Inc.

Dale Seymour Publications
2725 Sand Hill Road
Menlo Park, CA 94025
Customer Service: 800-872-1100

**DALE
SEYMOUR
PUBLICATIONS®**

Order number DS47052
ISBN 1-57232-805-3
30 -ML- 10 09

Printed on Recycled Paper

Contents

*Repeated-use sheet

*Repeated-use sheet

ONE-CENTIMETER GRAPH PAPER

1

3

Number Shape Clues

Find and record a number that fits each clue.

Draw one or more rectangles to show that your number fits the clue.

Record the factor pair that your rectangle shows.

Clues

1. You can make this number of tiles into a rectangle 2 tiles wide.

2. You can make this number of tiles into a rectangle 5 tiles wide.

3. You can make this number of tiles into *only* 1 rectangle.

4. You can make this number of tiles into a square.

5. You can make this number of tiles into *only* 2 rectangles.

6. You can make this number of tiles into at least 4 different rectangles.

Factor Pairs from 1 to 25

On the graph paper provided, draw rectangles to show the factor pairs for each number from 1 to 25. Label the dimensions of each rectangle and list the factor pair that each rectangle shows.

Below, record any observations or discoveries about the rectangles and factors for these numbers. (For example, which numbers have the most factors? The fewest? How many numbers have 2 as a factor?)

_____

_____

_____

_____

_____

_____

_____

_____

_____

_____

_____

To the Family

Factor Pairs from 1 to 25

Sessions 1–3

Math Content

Becoming familiar with factor pairs for the numbers 1–25 and the relationships among them

Materials

Student Sheet 2
3–5 sheets of one-centimeter graph paper
Pencil
Ruler (optional)

In class, we have been representing factor pairs as the dimensions of rectangular arrays and exploring the meaning of some mathematical terms such as *factor, multiple, prime,* and *square.*

For homework the next two nights, your child will use graph paper to draw rectangles that show the factor pairs for each number from 1 to 25. Your child will label the dimensions of each rectangle, list the factor pair that each rectangle shows, and record an observation or discovery about the rectangles and factors for these numbers. (For example, which numbers have the most factors? the fewest? How many numbers have 2 as a factor?)

13

Skip Counting

In the space below, record the first 20 numbers you would
say if you counted by a large one-digit number, such as 7 or
9, or a small two-digit number, such as 11 or 12. Try this
task without a calculator.

The number I chose to count by is _____.

The numbers I said were:

To the Family

Skip Counting

Sessions 1–3

Math Content
Developing understanding about multiples
Relating skip counting to multiplication

Materials
Student Sheet 3
Pencil
300 chart

To continue our class work with multiples, your child will skip count for homework, and record the first 20 numbers said when counting by either a large one-digit number, such as 7 or 9, or a small two-digit number, such as 11 or 12. For example, if you skip count by 3's, you will record 3, 6, 9, 12, 15 . . . 60.

1	2	3	4	5	6	7	8	9	10
11	12	13	14	15	16	17	18	19	20
21	22	23	24	25	26	27	28	29	30
31	32	33	34	35	36	37	38	39	40
41	42	43	44	45	46	47	48	49	50
51	52	53	54	55	56	57	58	59	60
61	62	63	64	65	66	67	68	69	70
71	72	73	74	75	76	77	78	79	80
81	82	83	84	85	86	87	88	89	90
91	92	93	94	95	96	97	98	99	100
101	102	103	104	105	106	107	108	109	110
111	112	113	114	115	116	117	118	119	120
121	122	123	124	125	126	127	128	129	130
131	132	133	134	135	136	137	138	139	140
141	142	143	144	145	146	147	148	149	150
151	152	153	154	155	156	157	158	159	160
161	162	163	164	165	166	167	168	169	170
171	172	173	174	175	176	177	178	179	180
181	182	183	184	185	186	187	188	189	190
191	192	193	194	195	196	197	198	199	200
201	202	203	204	205	206	207	208	209	210
211	212	213	214	215	216	217	218	219	220
221	222	223	224	225	226	227	228	229	230
231	232	233	234	235	236	237	238	239	240
241	242	243	244	245	246	247	248	249	250
251	252	253	254	255	256	257	258	259	260
261	262	263	264	265	266	267	268	269	270
271	272	273	274	275	276	277	278	279	280
281	282	283	284	285	286	287	288	289	290
291	292	293	294	295	296	297	298	299	300

Unit Resource
Mathematical Thinking at Grade 5

1	2	3	4	5	6	7	8	9	10
11	12	13	14	15	16	17	18	19	20
21	22	23	24	25	26	27	28	29	30
31	32	33	34	35	36	37	38	39	40
41	42	43	44	45	46	47	48	49	50
51	52	53	54	55	56	57	58	59	60
61	62	63	64	65	66	67	68	69	70
71	72	73	74	75	76	77	78	79	80
81	82	83	84	85	86	87	88	89	90
91	92	93	94	95	96	97	98	99	100
101	102	103	104	105	106	107	108	109	110
111	112	113	114	115	116	117	118	119	120
121	122	123	124	125	126	127	128	129	130
131	132	133	134	135	136	137	138	139	140
141	142	143	144	145	146	147	148	149	150
151	152	153	154	155	156	157	158	159	160
161	162	163	164	165	166	167	168	169	170
171	172	173	174	175	176	177	178	179	180
181	182	183	184	185	186	187	188	189	190
191	192	193	194	195	196	197	198	199	200
201	202	203	204	205	206	207	208	209	210
211	212	213	214	215	216	217	218	219	220
221	222	223	224	225	226	227	228	229	230
231	232	233	234	235	236	237	238	239	240
241	242	243	244	245	246	247	248	249	250
251	252	253	254	255	256	257	258	259	260
261	262	263	264	265	266	267	268	269	270
271	272	273	274	275	276	277	278	279	280
281	282	283	284	285	286	287	288	289	290
291	292	293	294	295	296	297	298	299	300

300 CHART

1	2	3	4	5	6	7	8	9	10
11	12	13	14	15	16	17	18	19	20
21	22	23	24	25	26	27	28	29	30
31	32	33	34	35	36	37	38	39	40
41	42	43	44	45	46	47	48	49	50
51	52	53	54	55	56	57	58	59	60
61	62	63	64	65	66	67	68	69	70
71	72	73	74	75	76	77	78	79	80
81	82	83	84	85	86	87	88	89	90
91	92	93	94	95	96	97	98	99	100
101	102	103	104	105	106	107	108	109	110
111	112	113	114	115	116	117	118	119	120
121	122	123	124	125	126	127	128	129	130
131	132	133	134	135	136	137	138	139	140
141	142	143	144	145	146	147	148	149	150
151	152	153	154	155	156	157	158	159	160
161	162	163	164	165	166	167	168	169	170
171	172	173	174	175	176	177	178	179	180
181	182	183	184	185	186	187	188	189	190
191	192	193	194	195	196	197	198	199	200
201	202	203	204	205	206	207	208	209	210
211	212	213	214	215	216	217	218	219	220
221	222	223	224	225	226	227	228	229	230
231	232	233	234	235	236	237	238	239	240
241	242	243	244	245	246	247	248	249	250
251	252	253	254	255	256	257	258	259	260
261	262	263	264	265	266	267	268	269	270
271	272	273	274	275	276	277	278	279	280
281	282	283	284	285	286	287	288	289	290
291	292	293	294	295	296	297	298	299	300

300 CHART

1	2	3	4	5	6	7	8	9	10
11	12	13	14	15	16	17	18	19	20
21	22	23	24	25	26	27	28	29	30
31	32	33	34	35	36	37	38	39	40
41	42	43	44	45	46	47	48	49	50
51	52	53	54	55	56	57	58	59	60
61	62	63	64	65	66	67	68	69	70
71	72	73	74	75	76	77	78	79	80
81	82	83	84	85	86	87	88	89	90
91	92	93	94	95	96	97	98	99	100
101	102	103	104	105	106	107	108	109	110
111	112	113	114	115	116	117	118	119	120
121	122	123	124	125	126	127	128	129	130
131	132	133	134	135	136	137	138	139	140
141	142	143	144	145	146	147	148	149	150
151	152	153	154	155	156	157	158	159	160
161	162	163	164	165	166	167	168	169	170
171	172	173	174	175	176	177	178	179	180
181	182	183	184	185	186	187	188	189	190
191	192	193	194	195	196	197	198	199	200
201	202	203	204	205	206	207	208	209	210
211	212	213	214	215	216	217	218	219	220
221	222	223	224	225	226	227	228	229	230
231	232	233	234	235	236	237	238	239	240
241	242	243	244	245	246	247	248	249	250
251	252	253	254	255	256	257	258	259	260
261	262	263	264	265	266	267	268	269	270
271	272	273	274	275	276	277	278	279	280
281	282	283	284	285	286	287	288	289	290
291	292	293	294	295	296	297	298	299	300

300 CHART

1	2	3	4	5	6	7	8	9	10
11	12	13	14	15	16	17	18	19	20
21	22	23	24	25	26	27	28	29	30
31	32	33	34	35	36	37	38	39	40
41	42	43	44	45	46	47	48	49	50
51	52	53	54	55	56	57	58	59	60
61	62	63	64	65	66	67	68	69	70
71	72	73	74	75	76	77	78	79	80
81	82	83	84	85	86	87	88	89	90
91	92	93	94	95	96	97	98	99	100
101	102	103	104	105	106	107	108	109	110
111	112	113	114	115	116	117	118	119	120
121	122	123	124	125	126	127	128	129	130
131	132	133	134	135	136	137	138	139	140
141	142	143	144	145	146	147	148	149	150
151	152	153	154	155	156	157	158	159	160
161	162	163	164	165	166	167	168	169	170
171	172	173	174	175	176	177	178	179	180
181	182	183	184	185	186	187	188	189	190
191	192	193	194	195	196	197	198	199	200
201	202	203	204	205	206	207	208	209	210
211	212	213	214	215	216	217	218	219	220
221	222	223	224	225	226	227	228	229	230
231	232	233	234	235	236	237	238	239	240
241	242	243	244	245	246	247	248	249	250
251	252	253	254	255	256	257	258	259	260
261	262	263	264	265	266	267	268	269	270
271	272	273	274	275	276	277	278	279	280
281	282	283	284	285	286	287	288	289	290
291	292	293	294	295	296	297	298	299	300

© Dale Seymour Publications®

27

1	2	3	4	5	6	7	8	9	10
11	12	13	14	15	16	17	18	19	20
21	22	23	24	25	26	27	28	29	30
31	32	33	34	35	36	37	38	39	40
41	42	43	44	45	46	47	48	49	50
51	52	53	54	55	56	57	58	59	60
61	62	63	64	65	66	67	68	69	70
71	72	73	74	75	76	77	78	79	80
81	82	83	84	85	86	87	88	89	90
91	92	93	94	95	96	97	98	99	100
101	102	103	104	105	106	107	108	109	110
111	112	113	114	115	116	117	118	119	120
121	122	123	124	125	126	127	128	129	130
131	132	133	134	135	136	137	138	139	140
141	142	143	144	145	146	147	148	149	150
151	152	153	154	155	156	157	158	159	160
161	162	163	164	165	166	167	168	169	170
171	172	173	174	175	176	177	178	179	180
181	182	183	184	185	186	187	188	189	190
191	192	193	194	195	196	197	198	199	200
201	202	203	204	205	206	207	208	209	210
211	212	213	214	215	216	217	218	219	220
221	222	223	224	225	226	227	228	229	230
231	232	233	234	235	236	237	238	239	240
241	242	243	244	245	246	247	248	249	250
251	252	253	254	255	256	257	258	259	260
261	262	263	264	265	266	267	268	269	270
271	272	273	274	275	276	277	278	279	280
281	282	283	284	285	286	287	288	289	290
291	292	293	294	295	296	297	298	299	300

Number Puzzle Recording Sheet

Check off each puzzle you solve. Record your answer.

Investigation 1 Number Puzzles

Puzzle	Answer
1	
2	
3	
4	
5	
6	
7	
8	

Puzzle	Answer
9☆	
10☆	
11☆	
12☆	
13☆	
14☆	

Save this recording sheet for use in Investigation 4.

Investigation 4 Number Puzzles

Puzzle	Answer
15	
16	
17	
18	
19	
20	
21	
22	

Puzzle	Answer
23☆	
24☆	
25☆	
26☆	
27☆	
28☆	

Make Your Own Puzzle

Here are three clues of a number puzzle:

My number is a multiple of 9.
My number is odd.
My number has two digits.

1. What numbers fit these three clues?

2. How did you find all the numbers that fit the clues?

3. Write a fourth clue that gives the puzzle just one answer.

4. What is the answer to your new puzzle?

What's the Number?

Three of these puzzles have more than one answer.
Try to find all the possible answers for each puzzle.
One of these puzzles is impossible.

1. My number is a factor of 20. It's also a factor of 30.

2. My number is a multiple of 10. It's a factor of 45.

3. My number is between 40 and 50. It is prime.

4. My number is a multiple of 4. It's a square number.
It's less than 50.

To the Family

What's the Number?

Sessions 4–6

Math Content
Reasoning about characteristics of numbers

Materials
Student Sheet 6
Pencil
300 chart

In class, we have been solving number puzzles which contain clues about numbers and number relationships. For example: My number is greater than 50, less than 100, a multiple of 15, and odd. What could my number be? For homework, your child will complete the puzzles on Student Sheet 6, What's the Number?

1	2	3	4	5	6	7	8	9	10
11	12	13	14	15	16	17	18	19	20
21	22	23	24	25	26	27	28	29	30
31	32	33	34	35	36	37	38	39	40
41	42	43	44	45	46	47	48	49	50
51	52	53	54	55	56	57	58	59	60
61	62	63	64	65	66	67	68	69	70
71	72	73	74	75	76	77	78	79	80
81	82	83	84	85	86	87	88	89	90
91	92	93	94	95	96	97	98	99	100
101	102	103	104	105	106	107	108	109	110
111	112	113	114	115	116	117	118	119	120
121	122	123	124	125	126	127	128	129	130
131	132	133	134	135	136	137	138	139	140
141	142	143	144	145	146	147	148	149	150
151	152	153	154	155	156	157	158	159	160
161	162	163	164	165	166	167	168	169	170
171	172	173	174	175	176	177	178	179	180
181	182	183	184	185	186	187	188	189	190
191	192	193	194	195	196	197	198	199	200
201	202	203	204	205	206	207	208	209	210
211	212	213	214	215	216	217	218	219	220
221	222	223	224	225	226	227	228	229	230
231	232	233	234	235	236	237	238	239	240
241	242	243	244	245	246	247	248	249	250
251	252	253	254	255	256	257	258	259	260
261	262	263	264	265	266	267	268	269	270
271	272	273	274	275	276	277	278	279	280
281	282	283	284	285	286	287	288	289	290
291	292	293	294	295	296	297	298	299	300

Make an Impossible Puzzle

Here are three clues of a number puzzle:

My number is less than 100.
My number is a multiple of 7.
My number is a multiple of 3.

1. What numbers fit these three clues?

2. How did you find all the numbers that fit the clues?

3. Write a fourth clue that makes the puzzle impossible.

4. Explain how you know your new puzzle is impossible.

To the Family

Make an Impossible Puzzle

Sessions 4–6

Math Content
Reasoning about characteristics of numbers

Materials
Student Sheet 7
Pencil
300 chart

Our class has continued to work on number puzzles. For homework, your child will solve a number puzzle, record the strategies involved, and add a clue which makes the puzzle impossible to solve. For example, if my number is a multiple of 15, has two digits, and is odd, the answers would be 45 and 75. If the final clue says that the number is less than 40 or the sum of the digits is more than 15, the puzzle would be impossible to solve.

1	2	3	4	5	6	7	8	9	10
11	12	13	14	15	16	17	18	19	20
21	22	23	24	25	26	27	28	29	30
31	32	33	34	35	36	37	38	39	40
41	42	43	44	45	46	47	48	49	50
51	52	53	54	55	56	57	58	59	60
61	62	63	64	65	66	67	68	69	70
71	72	73	74	75	76	77	78	79	80
81	82	83	84	85	86	87	88	89	90
91	92	93	94	95	96	97	98	99	100
101	102	103	104	105	106	107	108	109	110
111	112	113	114	115	116	117	118	119	120
121	122	123	124	125	126	127	128	129	130
131	132	133	134	135	136	137	138	139	140
141	142	143	144	145	146	147	148	149	150
151	152	153	154	155	156	157	158	159	160
161	162	163	164	165	166	167	168	169	170
171	172	173	174	175	176	177	178	179	180
181	182	183	184	185	186	187	188	189	190
191	192	193	194	195	196	197	198	199	200
201	202	203	204	205	206	207	208	209	210
211	212	213	214	215	216	217	218	219	220
221	222	223	224	225	226	227	228	229	230
231	232	233	234	235	236	237	238	239	240
241	242	243	244	245	246	247	248	249	250
251	252	253	254	255	256	257	258	259	260
261	262	263	264	265	266	267	268	269	270
271	272	273	274	275	276	277	278	279	280
281	282	283	284	285	286	287	288	289	290
291	292	293	294	295	296	297	298	299	300

Find the Counting Numbers

Find *all* the counting numbers that fit each clue.

1. If you count by this number, you will say 100,
   but you will *not* say 10.

2. If you count by this number, you will say 200,
   but you will *not* say 40.

3. If you count by this number, you will say 300,
   but you will *not* say 75.

To the Family

Find the Counting Numbers

Session 1

Math Content
Skip counting to develop an understanding of factors and multiples

Materials
Student Sheet 8
Pencil
300 chart

In class, we are extending our exploration of multiples and factors to include numbers up to 1000. One of the ways students become familiar with important numbers is by skip counting: 25, 50, 75 . . . 1000. For homework, your child will be solving puzzles that can be solved by skip counting.

1	2	3	4	5	6	7	8	9	10
11	12	13	14	15	16	17	18	19	20
21	22	23	24	25	26	27	28	29	30
31	32	33	34	35	36	37	38	39	40
41	42	43	44	45	46	47	48	49	50
51	52	53	54	55	56	57	58	59	60
61	62	63	64	65	66	67	68	69	70
71	72	73	74	75	76	77	78	79	80
81	82	83	84	85	86	87	88	89	90
91	92	93	94	95	96	97	98	99	100
101	102	103	104	105	106	107	108	109	110
111	112	113	114	115	116	117	118	119	120
121	122	123	124	125	126	127	128	129	130
131	132	133	134	135	136	137	138	139	140
141	142	143	144	145	146	147	148	149	150
151	152	153	154	155	156	157	158	159	160
161	162	163	164	165	166	167	168	169	170
171	172	173	174	175	176	177	178	179	180
181	182	183	184	185	186	187	188	189	190
191	192	193	194	195	196	197	198	199	200
201	202	203	204	205	206	207	208	209	210
211	212	213	214	215	216	217	218	219	220
221	222	223	224	225	226	227	228	229	230
231	232	233	234	235	236	237	238	239	240
241	242	243	244	245	246	247	248	249	250
251	252	253	254	255	256	257	258	259	260
261	262	263	264	265	266	267	268	269	270
271	272	273	274	275	276	277	278	279	280
281	282	283	284	285	286	287	288	289	290
291	292	293	294	295	296	297	298	299	300

53

1	2	3	4	5	6	7	8	9	10
11	12	13	14	15	16	17	18	19	20
21	22	23	24	25	26	27	28	29	30
31	32	33	34	35	36	37	38	39	40
41	42	43	44	45	46	47	48	49	50
51	52	53	54	55	56	57	58	59	60
61	62	63	64	65	66	67	68	69	70
71	72	73	74	75	76	77	78	79	80
81	82	83	84	85	86	87	88	89	90
91	92	93	94	95	96	97	98	99	100
101	102	103	104	105	106	107	108	109	110
111	112	113	114	115	116	117	118	119	120
121	122	123	124	125	126	127	128	129	130
131	132	133	134	135	136	137	138	139	140
141	142	143	144	145	146	147	148	149	150
151	152	153	154	155	156	157	158	159	160
161	162	163	164	165	166	167	168	169	170
171	172	173	174	175	176	177	178	179	180
181	182	183	184	185	186	187	188	189	190
191	192	193	194	195	196	197	198	199	200
201	202	203	204	205	206	207	208	209	210
211	212	213	214	215	216	217	218	219	220
221	222	223	224	225	226	227	228	229	230
231	232	233	234	235	236	237	238	239	240
241	242	243	244	245	246	247	248	249	250
251	252	253	254	255	256	257	258	259	260
261	262	263	264	265	266	267	268	269	270
271	272	273	274	275	276	277	278	279	280
281	282	283	284	285	286	287	288	289	290
291	292	293	294	295	296	297	298	299	300

© Dale Seymour Publications®

Unit Resource
Mathematical Thinking at Grade 5

300 CHART

1	2	3	4	5	6	7	8	9	10
11	12	13	14	15	16	17	18	19	20
21	22	23	24	25	26	27	28	29	30
31	32	33	34	35	36	37	38	39	40
41	42	43	44	45	46	47	48	49	50
51	52	53	54	55	56	57	58	59	60
61	62	63	64	65	66	67	68	69	70
71	72	73	74	75	76	77	78	79	80
81	82	83	84	85	86	87	88	89	90
91	92	93	94	95	96	97	98	99	100
101	102	103	104	105	106	107	108	109	110
111	112	113	114	115	116	117	118	119	120
121	122	123	124	125	126	127	128	129	130
131	132	133	134	135	136	137	138	139	140
141	142	143	144	145	146	147	148	149	150
151	152	153	154	155	156	157	158	159	160
161	162	163	164	165	166	167	168	169	170
171	172	173	174	175	176	177	178	179	180
181	182	183	184	185	186	187	188	189	190
191	192	193	194	195	196	197	198	199	200
201	202	203	204	205	206	207	208	209	210
211	212	213	214	215	216	217	218	219	220
221	222	223	224	225	226	227	228	229	230
231	232	233	234	235	236	237	238	239	240
241	242	243	244	245	246	247	248	249	250
251	252	253	254	255	256	257	258	259	260
261	262	263	264	265	266	267	268	269	270
271	272	273	274	275	276	277	278	279	280
281	282	283	284	285	286	287	288	289	290
291	292	293	294	295	296	297	298	299	300

15 × 20 GRID

15 × 20 GRID

15 × 20 GRID

67

More Factor Pairs

The multiple of 100 I have chosen is _____.

Find several factor pairs for the multiple of 100 you chose
and list them below.

_____

_____

_____

_____

_____

Write about the strategies you used to find the factor pairs.

To the Family

More Factor Pairs

Sessions 2–4

Math Content
Finding and relating factor pairs of multiples of 100

Materials
Student Sheet 9
Pencil

In class, we have been listing factor pairs of 100 and of multiples of 100, such as 1000 (10 × 100, 4 × 250, 50 × 20). For homework, your child will choose a multiple of 100 and find factor pairs for that number. Remind your child to bring this student sheet back to class so we can add to our class list.

Counting Backward

Choose a multiple of 100 and count backward by one of the factors on our class list of factor pairs.

The multiple I chose is _____.

The factor I am counting by is _____.

The numbers I said when I counted backward:

To the Family

Counting Backward

Sessions 2–4

Math Content
Becoming fluent with number sequences and patterns

Materials
Student Sheet 10
Pencil

In class, we are continuing our work with multiples and factors of numbers from 100 to 1000. For homework, your child will start at a multiple of 100 and count backward by one of the factors on the class factor pair list, recording the numbers on Student Sheet 10. For example if your child chooses 800 and elects to count by 40, the list would be: 760, 720, 680, 640, 600, 560, 520, 480, 440, 400, 360, 320, 280, 240, 200, 160, 120, 80, 40, 0.

What Could You Count By?

Choose a multiple of 100 (such as 300 or 500) or a multiple of 1000 (such as 2000 or 6000).

The multiple I chose is _____.

Find and record at least 5 different numbers you could count by so that somewhere in the count you would reach your chosen number.

How did you decide what numbers to try?

Number I tried that did not reach my multiple:

To the Family

What Could You Count By?

Session 1

Math Content
Skip-counting to find factors

Materials
Student Sheet 11
Pencil

Our work in class is focusing on using our knowledge of landmark, or special, numbers up to 1000 (including factors of 1000 and multiples of those factors) to explore landmarks up to 10,000. For homework, your child will choose a multiple of 100 or 1000 and find five numbers she or he can count by to reach that number. For example, you will land on 600 if you count by 75 (75, 150, 225, 300, 375, 450, 525, 600), 100 (100, 200, 300, 400, 500, 600) or 150 (150, 300, 450, 600). If you choose 6000, one number you count by is 1500. The sequence would be 1500, 3000, 4500, 6000.

Multiplication Clusters (page 1 of 2)

Use problems in the cluster to help you solve the last problem.
Add any other problems you use to help solve the last problem.

20×4	25×4
2×4	**23×4**

4×25	10×25
12×25	**13×25**

3×50	20×50
7×50	**17×50**

Multiplication Clusters (page 2 of 2)

Use problems in the cluster to help you solve the last problem.
Add any other problems you use to help solve the last problem.

30 × 5	200 × 5
233 × 10	**233 × 5**

4 × 25	10 × 25
40 × 25	50 × 25
6 × 25	**46 × 25**

500 × 4	1000 × 4
2500 × 4	**2507 × 4**

More Multiplication Clusters

Use problems in the cluster to help you solve the last problem.
Add any other problems you use to help solve the last problem.

8×25	30×25
40×25	**38×25**

25×40	70×10
75×40	**74×40**

25×4	200×4
250×4	275×4

$$277 \times 4$$

25×5	200×5
2000×5	**2025×5**

Challenging Multiplication Clusters

Use problems in the cluster to help you solve the last problem.
Add any other problems you use to help solve the last problem.

7 × 40	25 × 40
250 × 40	275 × 40

282 × 40

3 × 50	20 × 50
200 × 50	**197 × 50**

0.5 × 50	2.5 × 5
25 × 5	**2.5 × 50**

12 × 24	25 × 12
.5 × 24	**12.5 × 24**

Division Clusters

Use problems in the cluster to help you solve the last problem.
Add any other problems you use to help solve the last problem.

$$5 \div 5 \qquad\qquad 100 \div 5$$

$$30 \div 5 \qquad\qquad \mathbf{135 \div 5}$$

$$24 \div 4 \qquad\qquad 100 \div 4$$

$$200 \div 4 \qquad\qquad 224 \div 4$$

$$\mathbf{248 \div 4}$$

$$100 \div 20 \qquad\qquad 1000 \div 20$$

$$800 \div 20 \qquad\qquad \mathbf{900 \div 20}$$

More Division Clusters

Use problems in the cluster to help you solve the last problem.
Add any other problems you use to help solve the last problem.

$100 \div 4$	$16 \div 4$
$116 \div 4$	**$232 \div 4$**

$100 \div 2$	$200 \div 2$
$90 \div 2$	$10 \div 2$
$190 \div 2$	

$100 \div 25$	$1000 \div 25$
$2000 \div 25$	$300 \div 25$
$2300 \div 25$	

Challenging Division Clusters

Use problems in the cluster to help you solve the last problem.
Add any other problems you use to help solve the last problem.

$100 \div 50$	$1000 \div 5$
$10,000 \div 50$	**$10,100 \div 50$**

$100 \div 25$	$1000 \div 25$
$500 \div 25$	$10,000 \div 25$
	$10,500 \div 25$

$500 \div 50$	$1000 \div 50$
$2000 \div 50$	**$2500 \div 50$**

$2000 \div 400$	$8000 \div 400$
$4,000 \div 400$	**$20,000 \div 400$**

Writing About Multiplication Clusters

Solve each cluster. Add to the cluster any other problem(s) you used to solve the last problem. Write about how you used the problems in the cluster to solve the final problem.

5×20 10×20

50×20 60×20

65×20

3×25 40×25

80×25 77×25

To the Family

Writing About Multiplication Clusters

Sessions 2–4

Math Content
Developing strategies that rely on landmarks up to 10,000 for solving
 multiplication and division problems

Materials
Student Sheet 18
Pencil

In class, we have been solving cluster problems—sets of problems that
help students think about using what they know to solve harder problems. For example, what do you know that would help you solve $12 \times$
25? If you know $10 \times 25 = 250$, then you can start with 250 and add two
more 25's to get 300. If you know that $4 \times 25 = 100$, then you can think
of 12×25 as $4 \times 25 + 4 \times 25 + 4 \times 25$, or $100 + 100 + 100$. As students
work with the clusters on Student Sheet 18, they are learning to think
about and use all the number relationships they know that might help
them solve the problem they are working on.

Make Your Own Cluster

Write a cluster of problems to help you solve one of the
following problems.

47×40 $336 \div 4$

Record your cluster below. Write about how the problems
in the cluster helped you solve the original problem.

To the Family

Make Your Own Cluster

Sessions 2–4

Math Content
Developing strategies that rely on landmarks up to 10,000 for solving
multiplication and division problems

Materials
Student Sheet 19
Pencil

To continue our work with clusters, your child will make up a set of cluster problems for one of the problems listed on Student Sheet 19 and
write about how the problems in the cluster helped solve the original
problem.

Factor Pairs of 950

Find factor pairs of 950 and write about how you found
each pair.

To the Family

Factor Pairs of 950

Session 5

Math Content

Finding factor pairs of a number
Using knowledge of related factor pairs and number relationships

Materials

Student Sheet 20
Pencil

In class, students have been working to explain their mathematical thinking and reasoning clearly, both orally and in writing. For homework, students will find factor pairs of 950 and write about how they found each factor pair.

How to Play Close to 1000

Materials

- One deck of Numeral Cards
- Close to 1000 Score Sheet for each player

Players: 1, 2, or 3

How to Play

1. Deal out eight Numeral Cards to each player.

2. Use any six cards to make two numbers. For example, a 6, a 5, and a 2 could make 652, 625, 526, 562, 256, or 265. Wild Cards can be used as any numeral. Try to make two numbers that, when added, give you a total that is close to 1000.

3. Write these numbers and their total on the Close to 1000 Score Sheet. For example: 652 + 347 = 999.

4. Find your score. Your score is the difference between your total and 1000.

5. Put the cards you used in a discard pile. Keep the two cards you didn't use for the next round.

6. For the next round, deal six new cards to each player. Make more numbers that come close to 1000. When you run out of cards, mix up the discard pile and use them again.

7. After five rounds, total your scores. Lowest score wins.

Scoring Variation Write the score with plus and minus signs to show the direction of your total away from 1000. For example: If your total is 999, your score is –1. If your total is 1005, your score is +5. The total of these two scores would be +4. Your goal is to get a total score for five rounds that is close to 0.

To the Family

Close to 1000 and Close to 0

Session 1

Math Content
Developing strategies for adding and subtracting 3- and 4-digit numbers

Materials
Student Sheets 21, 22, 23, and 24
Numeral Cards (pages 1–3)
Scissors for cutting Numeral Cards apart into decks
Envelope or plastic bag for storing the deck of Numeral Cards (optional)

In class, we have been playing Close to 1000 and Close to 0, games that involve adding and subtracting 3- and 4-digit numbers. For homework, your child will teach the games to someone at home and then play a few rounds.

0	0	1	1
0	0	1	1
2	2	3	3
2	2	3	3

4	4	5	5
4	4	5	5
6	6	7	7
6	6	7	7

8	8	9	9
8	8	9	9
WILD CARD	WILD CARD		
WILD CARD	WILD CARD		

Close to 1000 Score Sheet

Game 1   Score

Round 1: __ __ __ + __ __ __ = _____   _____

Round 2: __ __ __ + __ __ __ = _____   _____

Round 3: __ __ __ + __ __ __ = _____   _____

Round 4: __ __ __ + __ __ __ = _____   _____

Round 5: __ __ __ + __ __ __ = _____   _____

TOTAL SCORE   _____

Game 2   Score

Round 1: __ __ __ + __ __ __ = _____   _____

Round 2: __ __ __ + __ __ __ = _____   _____

Round 3: __ __ __ + __ __ __ = _____   _____

Round 4: __ __ __ + __ __ __ = _____   _____

Round 5: __ __ __ + __ __ __ = _____   _____

TOTAL SCORE   _____

How to Play Close to 0

Materials

- One deck of Numeral Cards
- Close to 0 Score Sheet for each player

Players: 1, 2, or 3

How to Play

1. Deal out eight Numeral Cards to each player.

2. Use any six cards to make two numbers. For example, a 6, a 5, and a 2 could make 652, 625, 526, 562, 256, or 265. Wild Cards can be used as any numeral. Try to make two numbers that, when subtracted, give you a difference that is close to 0.

3. Write these numbers and their difference on the Close to 0 Score Sheet. For example: 652 – 647 = 5. The difference is your score.

4. Put the cards you used in a discard pile. Keep the two cards you didn't use for the next round.

5. For the next round, deal six new cards to each player. Make two more numbers with a difference close to 0. When you run out of cards, mix up the discard pile and use them again.

6. After five rounds, total your scores. Lowest score wins.

To the Family

Close to 1000 and Close to 0

Session 1

Math Content
Developing strategies for adding and subtracting 3- and 4-digit numbers

Materials
Student Sheets 21, 22, 23, and 24
Numeral Cards (pages 1–3)
Scissors for cutting Numeral Cards apart into decks
Envelope or plastic bag for storing the deck of Numeral Cards (optional)

In class, we have been playing Close to 1000 and Close to 0, games that involve adding and subtracting 3- and 4-digit numbers. For homework, your child will teach the games to someone at home and then play a few rounds.

Close to 0 Score Sheet

Game 1   Score

Round 1:   __ __ __ − __ __ __ = _____   _____

Round 2:   __ __ __ − __ __ __ = _____   _____

Round 3:   __ __ __ − __ __ __ = _____   _____

Round 4:   __ __ __ − __ __ __ = _____   _____

Round 5:   __ __ __ − __ __ __ = _____   _____

                                 TOTAL SCORE   _____

Game 2   Score

Round 1:   __ __ __ − __ __ __ = _____   _____

Round 2:   __ __ __ − __ __ __ = _____   _____

Round 3:   __ __ __ − __ __ __ = _____   _____

Round 4:   __ __ __ − __ __ __ = _____   _____

Round 5:   __ __ __ − __ __ __ = _____   _____

                                 TOTAL SCORE   _____

0	0	1	1
0	0	1	1
2	2	3	3
2	2	3	3

4	4	5	5
4	4	5	5
<u>6</u>	<u>6</u>	7	7
<u>6</u>	<u>6</u>	7	7

8	8	9	9
8	8	9	9
WILD CARD	WILD CARD		
WILD CARD	WILD CARD		

Investigation 4 • Resource
Mathematical Thinking at Grade 5

Close to 1000 Score Sheet

Game 1   Score

Round 1:   __ __ __ + __ __ __ = _____   _____

Round 2:   __ __ __ + __ __ __ = _____   _____

Round 3:   __ __ __ + __ __ __ = _____   _____

Round 4:   __ __ __ + __ __ __ = _____   _____

Round 5:   __ __ __ + __ __ __ = _____   _____

                                                  TOTAL SCORE   _____

Game 2   Score

Round 1:   __ __ __ + __ __ __ = _____   _____

Round 2:   __ __ __ + __ __ __ = _____   _____

Round 3:   __ __ __ + __ __ __ = _____   _____

Round 4:   __ __ __ + __ __ __ = _____   _____

Round 5:   __ __ __ + __ __ __ = _____   _____

                                                  TOTAL SCORE   _____

To the Family

Close to 1000 and Close to 0

Session 1

Math Content
Developing strategies for adding and subtracting 3- and 4-digit numbers

Materials
Student Sheets 21, 22, 23, and 24
Numeral Cards (pages 1–3)
Scissors for cutting Numeral Cards apart into decks
Envelope or plastic bag for storing the deck of Numeral Cards (optional)

In class, we have been playing Close to 1000 and Close to 0, games that involve adding and subtracting 3- and 4-digit numbers. For homework, your child will teach the games to someone at home and then play a few rounds.

Close to 1000 Score Sheet

+---+
| **Game 1**   Score |
| |
| Round 1: __ __ __ + __ __ __ = _____   _____ |
| |
| Round 2: __ __ __ + __ __ __ = _____   _____ |
| |
| Round 3: __ __ __ + __ __ __ = _____   _____ |
| |
| Round 4: __ __ __ + __ __ __ = _____   _____ |
| |
| Round 5: __ __ __ + __ __ __ = _____   _____ |
| |
| TOTAL SCORE   _____ |
+---+

+---+
| **Game 2**   Score |
| |
| Round 1: __ __ __ + __ __ __ = _____   _____ |
| |
| Round 2: __ __ __ + __ __ __ = _____   _____ |
| |
| Round 3: __ __ __ + __ __ __ = _____   _____ |
| |
| Round 4: __ __ __ + __ __ __ = _____   _____ |
| |
| Round 5: __ __ __ + __ __ __ = _____   _____ |
| |
| TOTAL SCORE   _____ |
+---+

To the Family

Close to 1000 and Close to 0

Session 1

Math Content
Developing strategies for adding and subtracting 3- and 4-digit numbers

Materials
Student Sheets 21, 22, 23, and 24
Numeral Cards (pages 1–3)
Scissors for cutting Numeral Cards apart into decks
Envelope or plastic bag for storing the deck of Numeral Cards (optional)

In class, we have been playing Close to 1000 and Close to 0, games that involve adding and subtracting 3- and 4-digit numbers. For homework, your child will teach the games to someone at home and then play a few rounds.

Close to 0 Score Sheet

Game 1   Score

Round 1: ___ ___ ___ – ___ ___ ___ = _____   _____

Round 2: ___ ___ ___ – ___ ___ ___ = _____   _____

Round 3: ___ ___ ___ – ___ ___ ___ = _____   _____

Round 4: ___ ___ ___ – ___ ___ ___ = _____   _____

Round 5: ___ ___ ___ – ___ ___ ___ = _____   _____

TOTAL SCORE _____

Game 2   Score

Round 1: ___ ___ ___ – ___ ___ ___ = _____   _____

Round 2: ___ ___ ___ – ___ ___ ___ = _____   _____

Round 3: ___ ___ ___ – ___ ___ ___ = _____   _____

Round 4: ___ ___ ___ – ___ ___ ___ = _____   _____

Round 5: ___ ___ ___ – ___ ___ ___ = _____   _____

TOTAL SCORE _____

To the Family

Close to 1000 and Close to 0

Session 1

Math Content
Developing strategies for adding and subtracting 3- and 4-digit numbers

Materials
Student Sheets 21, 22, 23, and 24
Numeral Cards (pages 1–3)
Scissors for cutting Numeral Cards apart into decks
Envelope or plastic bag for storing the deck of Numeral Cards (optional)

In class, we have been playing Close to 1000 and Close to 0, games that involve adding and subtracting 3- and 4-digit numbers. For homework, your child will teach the games to someone at home and then play a few rounds.

Close to 0 Score Sheet

Game 1   Score

Round 1:   __ __ __ – __ __ __ = _____   _____

Round 2:   __ __ __ – __ __ __ = _____   _____

Round 3:   __ __ __ – __ __ __ = _____   _____

Round 4:   __ __ __ – __ __ __ = _____   _____

Round 5:   __ __ __ – __ __ __ = _____   _____

TOTAL SCORE   _____

Game 2   Score

Round 1:   __ __ __ – __ __ __ = _____   _____

Round 2:   __ __ __ – __ __ __ = _____   _____

Round 3:   __ __ __ – __ __ __ = _____   _____

Round 4:   __ __ __ – __ __ __ = _____   _____

Round 5:   __ __ __ – __ __ __ = _____   _____

TOTAL SCORE   _____

To the Family

Close to 1000 and Close to 0

Session 1

Math Content

Developing strategies for adding and subtracting 3- and 4-digit numbers

Materials

Student Sheets 21, 22, 23, and 24
Numeral Cards (pages 1–3)
Scissors for cutting Numeral Cards apart into decks
Envelope or plastic bag for storing the deck of Numeral Cards (optional)

In class, we have been playing Close to 1000 and Close to 0, games that involve adding and subtracting 3- and 4-digit numbers. For homework, your child will teach the games to someone at home and then play a few rounds.

Many Squares Poster Tasks (Group A)

1. Label these squares on the poster:

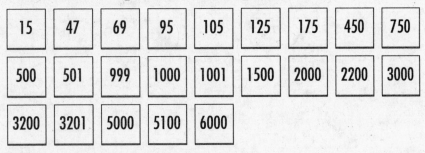

| 15 | 47 | 69 | 95 | 105 | 125 | 175 | 450 | 750 |

| 500 | 501 | 999 | 1000 | 1001 | 1500 | 2000 | 2200 | 3000 |

| 3200 | 3201 | 5000 | 5100 | 6000 |

2. Find each number described below. Label the square on the poster, and record the number on this sheet.

What number is . . .

1 row below 750? _____

2 rows below 750? _____

5 rows below 750? _____

10 rows below 750? _____

20 rows below 750? _____

3. Find each number described below. Label the square on the poster, and record the number on this sheet.

What number is . . .

25 more than 5725? _____

50 more than 5725? _____

53 more than 5725? _____

100 more than 5725? _____

1000 more than 5725? _____

100 less than 5725? _____

150 less than 5725? _____

Many Squares Poster Tasks (Group B)

1. Label these squares on the poster:

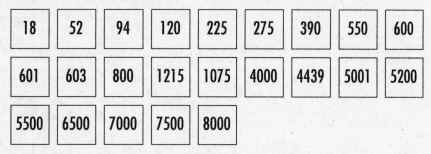

| 18 | 52 | 94 | 120 | 225 | 275 | 390 | 550 | 600 |

| 601 | 603 | 800 | 1215 | 1075 | 4000 | 4439 | 5001 | 5200 |

| 5500 | 6500 | 7000 | 7500 | 8000 |

2. Find each number described below. Label the square on the poster, and record the number on this sheet.

What number is . . .

1 row below 1075? _____

2 rows below 1075? _____

5 rows below 1075? _____

10 rows below 1075? _____

20 rows below 1075? _____

3. Find each number described below. Label the square on the poster, and record the number on this sheet.

What number is . . .

25 more than 6050? _____

50 more than 6050? _____

53 more than 6050? _____

100 more than 6050? _____

1000 more than 6050? _____

100 less than 6050? _____

150 less than 6050? _____

Many Squares Poster Tasks (Group C)

1. Label these squares on the poster:

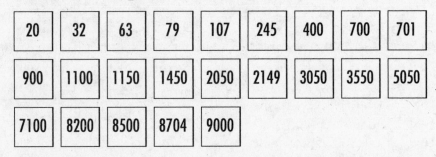

2. Find each number described below. Label the square
on the poster, and record the number on this sheet.

What number is . . .

2 rows below 1150? _____

4 rows below 1150? _____

5 rows below 1150? _____

10 rows below 1150? _____

20 rows below 1150? _____

3. Find each number described below. Label the square
on the poster, and record the number on this sheet.

What number is . . .

25 more than 9525? _____

50 more than 9525? _____

53 more than 9525? _____

100 more than 9525? _____

100 less than 9525? _____

150 less than 9525? _____

1000 less than 9525? _____

Many Squares Poster Tasks (Group D)

1. Label these squares on the poster:

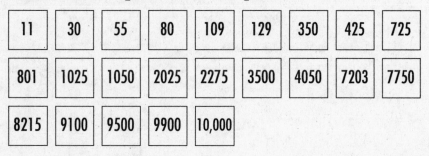

11	30	55	80	109	129	350	425	725
801	1025	1050	2025	2275	3500	4050	7203	7750
8215	9100	9500	9900	10,000				

2. Find each number described below. Label the square on the poster, and record the number on this sheet.

What number is . . .

2 rows above 10,000? _____

3 rows above 10,000? _____

4 rows above 10,000? _____

11 rows above 10,000? _____

5500 less than 10,000? _____

3. Find each number described below. Label the square on the poster, and record the number on this sheet.

What number is . . .

25 more than 3250? _____

50 more than 3250? _____

53 more than 3250? _____

100 more than 3250? _____

2000 more than 3250? _____

25 less than 3250? _____

75 less than 3250? _____

Exploring the Many Squares Poster

1. What are the numbers of the squares in the box marked with triangles? (Write the numbers here. Do *not* label these squares on your poster.)

2. How many squares are in the box marked with stars? _____

   How many squares on the poster are *not* in the box marked with stars? _____

   How do you know?

3. How many squares are in the box marked with dots? _____

   How many squares on the poster are *not* in the box marked with dots? _____

   How do you know?

4. What advice would you give someone who wanted to find 8250 on the poster?

1	2	3	4	5	6	7	8	9	10
11	12	13	14	15	16	17	18	19	20
21	22	23	24	25	26	27	28	29	30
31	32	33	34	35	36	37	38	39	40
41	42	43	44	45	46	47	48	49	50
51	52	53	54	55	56	57	58	59	60
61	62	63	64	65	66	67	68	69	70
71	72	73	74	75	76	77	78	79	80
81	82	83	84	85	86	87	88	89	90
91	92	93	94	95	96	97	98	99	100
101	102	103	104	105	106	107	108	109	110
111	112	113	114	115	116	117	118	119	120
121	122	123	124	125	126	127	128	129	130
131	132	133	134	135	136	137	138	139	140
141	142	143	144	145	146	147	148	149	150
151	152	153	154	155	156	157	158	159	160
161	162	163	164	165	166	167	168	169	170
171	172	173	174	175	176	177	178	179	180
181	182	183	184	185	186	187	188	189	190
191	192	193	194	195	196	197	198	199	200
201	202	203	204	205	206	207	208	209	210
211	212	213	214	215	216	217	218	219	220
221	222	223	224	225	226	227	228	229	230
231	232	233	234	235	236	237	238	239	240
241	242	243	244	245	246	247	248	249	250
251	252	253	254	255	256	257	258	259	260
261	262	263	264	265	266	267	268	269	270
271	272	273	274	275	276	277	278	279	280
281	282	283	284	285	286	287	288	289	290
291	292	293	294	295	296	297	298	299	300

1	2	3	4	5	6	7	8	9	10
11	12	13	14	15	16	17	18	19	20
21	22	23	24	25	26	27	28	29	30
31	32	33	34	35	36	37	38	39	40
41	42	43	44	45	46	47	48	49	50
51	52	53	54	55	56	57	58	59	60
61	62	63	64	65	66	67	68	69	70
71	72	73	74	75	76	77	78	79	80
81	82	83	84	85	86	87	88	89	90
91	92	93	94	95	96	97	98	99	100
101	102	103	104	105	106	107	108	109	110
111	112	113	114	115	116	117	118	119	120
121	122	123	124	125	126	127	128	129	130
131	132	133	134	135	136	137	138	139	140
141	142	143	144	145	146	147	148	149	150
151	152	153	154	155	156	157	158	159	160
161	162	163	164	165	166	167	168	169	170
171	172	173	174	175	176	177	178	179	180
181	182	183	184	185	186	187	188	189	190
191	192	193	194	195	196	197	198	199	200
201	202	203	204	205	206	207	208	209	210
211	212	213	214	215	216	217	218	219	220
221	222	223	224	225	226	227	228	229	230
231	232	233	234	235	236	237	238	239	240
241	242	243	244	245	246	247	248	249	250
251	252	253	254	255	256	257	258	259	260
261	262	263	264	265	266	267	268	269	270
271	272	273	274	275	276	277	278	279	280
281	282	283	284	285	286	287	288	289	290
291	292	293	294	295	296	297	298	299	300

Problems from Close to 1000

Suppose you are dealt these hands in Close to 1000.
What numbers would you make for the best score?
(Best score = sum as close to 1000 as possible)

Score

Round 1 | 4 | 6 | 0 | 5 | 3 | 2 | 7 | 9 |

_____ + _____ = _____   _____

Round 2 | 2 | 8 | 4 | 4 | 7 | 2 | 1 | 4 |

_____ + _____ = _____   _____

Round 3 | 3 | 7 | 1 | 9 | 6 | 0 | 5 | 3 |

_____ + _____ = _____   _____

Round 4 | 8 | 5 | 0 | 3 | 0 | 1 | 4 | 2 |

_____ + _____ = _____   _____

Round 5 | 0 | 5 | 6 | 3 | 7 | 4 | 2 | 1 |

_____ + _____ = _____   _____

TOTAL SCORE _____

To the Family

Problems from Close to 1000

Sessions 2–4

Math Content
Developing strategies for adding and subtracting 3- and 4-digit numbers

Materials
Student Sheet 27
Numeral Cards
Pencil

To continue practicing the strategies they are developing to add and subtract numbers, students will complete the problems on Student Sheet 27, which are based on the game Close to 1000.

Problems from Close to 0

Suppose you are dealt these hands in a game of Close to 0.
What numbers would you make for the best score?
(Best score = difference as close to 0 as possible)

Score

Round 1 | 5 | 3 | <u>6</u> | <u>9</u> | 0 | <u>6</u> | 2 | 1 |

_____ − _____ = _____ _____

Round 2 | 4 | 8 | 1 | 5 | 7 | 2 | 8 | <u>6</u> |

_____ − _____ = _____ _____

Round 3 | 1 | 0 | 1 | 5 | <u>9</u> | 0 | 2 | <u>6</u> |

_____ − _____ = _____ _____

Round 4 | <u>6</u> | 2 | 3 | 2 | 4 | 8 | 5 | 0 |

_____ − _____ = _____ _____

Round 5 | 8 | 4 | 0 | 2 | 7 | 3 | <u>9</u> | 1 |

_____ − _____ = _____ _____

TOTAL SCORE _____

To the Family

Problems from Close to 0

Sessions 2–4

Math Content
Developing strategies for adding and subtracting 3- and 4-digit numbers

Materials
Student Sheet 28
Numeral Cards
Pencil

To continue practicing the strategies they are developing, students will complete the problems on Student Sheet 28, which are based on the game Close to 0.

Add a Clue

Here are three clues of a number puzzle:

My number is a factor of 1000.

My number is a multiple of 25.

My number is a factor of 300.

1. What numbers fit these three clues?

2. How did you find the numbers that fit the clues?

3. Write a fourth clue that gives the puzzle just one answer. Do *not* use a clue about what the number is greater than, and do *not* use a clue about what the number is less than.

4. What is the answer to your new puzzle? How do you know?

1	2	3	4	5	6	7	8	9	10
11	12	13	14	15	16	17	18	19	20
21	22	23	24	25	26	27	28	29	30
31	32	33	34	35	36	37	38	39	40
41	42	43	44	45	46	47	48	49	50
51	52	53	54	55	56	57	58	59	60
61	62	63	64	65	66	67	68	69	70
71	72	73	74	75	76	77	78	79	80
81	82	83	84	85	86	87	88	89	90
91	92	93	94	95	96	97	98	99	100
101	102	103	104	105	106	107	108	109	110
111	112	113	114	115	116	117	118	119	120
121	122	123	124	125	126	127	128	129	130
131	132	133	134	135	136	137	138	139	140
141	142	143	144	145	146	147	148	149	150
151	152	153	154	155	156	157	158	159	160
161	162	163	164	165	166	167	168	169	170
171	172	173	174	175	176	177	178	179	180
181	182	183	184	185	186	187	188	189	190
191	192	193	194	195	196	197	198	199	200
201	202	203	204	205	206	207	208	209	210
211	212	213	214	215	216	217	218	219	220
221	222	223	224	225	226	227	228	229	230
231	232	233	234	235	236	237	238	239	240
241	242	243	244	245	246	247	248	249	250
251	252	253	254	255	256	257	258	259	260
261	262	263	264	265	266	267	268	269	270
271	272	273	274	275	276	277	278	279	280
281	282	283	284	285	286	287	288	289	290
291	292	293	294	295	296	297	298	299	300

Another Add a Clue

Here are three clues of a number puzzle:

My number is a factor of 3000.
My number is a factor of 50.
My number is a factor of 900.

1. What numbers fit these three clues?

2. How did you find the numbers that fit the clues?

3. Write a fourth clue that gives the puzzle just one answer. *Do not* use a clue about what the number is greater than, and *do not* use a clue about what the number is less than.

4. What is the answer to your new puzzle? How do you know?

To the Family

Another Add a Clue

Sessions 5–6

Math Content
Reasoning about factors of 1000 and 10,000 and multiples of
these factors

Materials
Student Sheet 30
Pencil

In class, we have been thinking about factors and multiples of larger
numbers, such as 1000 and 10,000. For homework, your child will solve
the puzzle on Student Sheet 30 which involves reasoning about the factors of 1000 and 10,000 and the multiples of those factors.

Practice Page A

Solve this problem in two different ways, and write about
how you solved it:

  $307 - 289 =$

Here is the first way I solved it:

Here is the second way I solved it:

Practice Page B

Solve this problem in two different ways, and write about
how you solved it:

$$354 + 534 =$$

Here is the first way I solved it:

Here is the second way I solved it:

Practice Page C

Solve this problem in two different ways, and write about
how you solved it:

$$42 \times 19 =$$

Here is the first way I solved it:

Here is the second way I solved it:

Practice Page D

Solve this problem in two different ways, and write about
how you solved it:

789 + 1038 =

Here is the first way I solved it:

Here is the second way I solved it:

Practice Page E

Solve this problem in two different ways, and write about how you solved it:

$$104 \div 8 =$$

Here is the first way I solved it:

Here is the second way I solved it:

Practice Page F

In our classroom we have 4 bookcases. Each bookcase has 4 shelves. On each shelf there are 10 books. How many books do we have in our classroom?

Show how you solved this problem. You can use numbers, words, or pictures.

Practice Page G

We have 140 music cassettes that we want to sell at the flea market. We will put 14 cassettes in each bag to sell. How many bags of cassettes will we have?

Show how you solved this problem. You can use numbers, words, or pictures.

Practice Page H

My friend has 24 pencils in a box. She wants to divide them equally among herself, her sister, and me. How many pencils will we each get?

Show how you solved this problem. You can use numbers, words, or pictures.